CONTENTS

FOREWORD

Luke, a Gentile Christian writing for those who did not have a Jewish background, teaches nothing that is not in the other Gospels. He has, however, his own distinctive emphasis. Thus in teaching that Christ's Gospel is addressed to all, he teaches that which is common to all the Gospels. He, however, stresses this aspect of the Gospel message particularly strongly. He traces the origin of Christ to Adam: Matthew traces it to Abraham. Also, he brings out the universal scope of the Gospel in stories that he alone relates. He makes the Samaritans models of charity (10:25-27; 17:11-19), and the Gentiles models of good conduct and great faith (7:9). He stresses that Christ went about doing good not only for his own people but for all, even those whom the Jews considered unacceptable outsiders. An aspect of the universal theme is the emphasis on the role and dignity of women. More women appear in his Gospel than in the others and the widow in the parable in Chapter 15 stands for God. This is something quite remarkable in Jewish literature.

Luke gives his own distinct thrust to Christ's teaching that he came to save and not to damn sinners. This teaching is conveyed in a number of parables peculiar to Luke: the parables of the lost sheep and the lost drachma (15), the sinful woman (7:36-50), of patience with the barren fig tree (16:19-31), of the Pharisee and the publican (18:10-14), the story of Zacchaeus (19:1-10), and the promise to the 'good thief' on the Cross (23:43). In order to paint a picture of Christ who came to lift burdens, to heal and to save, he omits some harsh sayings reported in Mark, his principal source (Mk 4:12; 9:42-48; 14:21).

The spirit of joy pervades the whole of Luke's Gospel. Luke notes that the coming of salvation creates an atmosphere of joy;

unsurprisingly he supplies the Joyful Mysteries of the Rosary. He has written the Gospel of Prayer. Jesus is shown praying before all his major decisions and we have in Chapter 11 a marvellous account to Our Lord's teaching on prayer.

Luke puts strongly the teaching of Christ on poverty and the poor. His is the Gospel for and on the poor, as is clear in material that is proper to him: the parable of Dives and Lazarus (16:19-31), of the rich fool (12:13-21) and the command to invite the poor to one's parties (14:12-14). The 'option for the poor' is writ large in this Gospel. Writ large, too, is the warning against attachment to the riches of this world, as spelled out in his version of the Beatitudes.

Luke's Gospel is a celebration of Christ's joyful message that He has come to save and to heal, to lift burdens, not impose them, to show compassion and not to condemn, to see all as friends to be won and never as enemies to be confounded.

LUKE IN POETRY

> When I re-read the Gospel I compare it
> To walking through a beautiful countryside:
> Each time I walk I see the same landscape,
> But nature, never idle, has painted
> Some hill or mountain with fresh colour,
> Or outlined more clearly the shape
> Of a deep blue lake, or flooded
> To a foaming cataract
> The placid, meandering summer stream.
> (Jesus Heals a Crippled Woman)

Bernadette Quinn's poems are a celebration of Luke's Gospel, its themes and teaching, its personalities and their actions. They bring us through the Gospel, situating Christ's planting of the seed and the diverse responses in a fresh perspective. They delineate the central and peripheral characters, and at the centre is Christ proclaiming in word and deed the joyful fact that the Spirit is at work around us, in us, and will be with us to the end of time. The poems highlight the call of Christ to follow his path. They invite us to re-read the Gospel so that

> New meanings come to light,
> New insights brighten up the pages,
> Which make me pause, to reflect…
> *(Jesus Heals a Crippled Woman)*

These are prayer poems born of contemplation. They invite us not simply to read the text or study it objectively; rather they call us to enter imaginatively into the episodes of the Gospel, questioning the characters and undergoing the same experiences as they did.

> The danger became so great
> That your disciples woke you up
> With screams of terror,
> Their terror, I imagine, not expressed
> In words of gentleness
> But in screams accompanied by hysterically
> Shaking you awake.
>
> Then the question was put to your friends:
> 'Where is your faith?'
> Yes, where indeed is *our* faith
> When the wind and the storm
> Rock the boat that is our Church?
> *(Jesus Calms a Storm)*

There is here, as throughout the poems, the application of Christ's teaching to our own lives:

> Careless parenting, religious leaders
> Unfaithful to their vocation,
> Unjust employers, dishonest employees,
> Corrupt political leaders,
> Ungrateful and neglectful children –
> Each of us has to answer to God
> For our failures to use our talents
> In the roles allotted to us.
> *(Faithful and Unfaithful Servants)*

Underlying all is Luke's sense of joy linked to prayer:

> Above all they give us the joy
> Of knowing that we are loved by God,
> And being so loved we must extend
> This love that envelops us to others,
> Regardless of religion
> Social or other differences,
> And by acting thus we are helping in the work
> Of building the Kingdom of God.
> *(Moments with God)*

These poems call us to come and see, and savour the sweetness of the Lord's company and its energising power.

Noel Barber, SJ
Milltown Park,
4 October 1999

AN ANGEL VISITS ZECHARIAH

Zechariah, why did you doubt the angel's word?
You were a God-fearing man, always ready
To do your duty in the Temple of the Lord,
And it was while you were serving him faithfully
He saw fit to interrupt your work
With this extraordinary message:
'Your wife will bear you a son.'

Because Elizabeth was old and childless
And you, yourself, advanced in years,
You could not believe this could happen,
Thus limiting the power of God.

Because of your unbelief, the angel
Deprived you of the power of speech,
And in that state you would remain
Until the Lord's promise
Would be fulfilled.

THE BIRTH OF JESUS IS ANNOUNCED

Even now, after two thousand years,
Can we fully absorb that great event
When Gabriel appeared to you, Mary,
And greeted you with these astonishing words:
'The Lord is with you and has greatly blessed you!'

Where were you when the angel spoke?
Were you going about your daily work?
Were you deep in prayer or
Preparing some loving, thoughtful act
For an elderly neighbour
Or a sick and lonely friend?

The Lord had always been with you
But from this day forth
Your life would never be the same.
Though greatly troubled and afraid
You accepted the angel's explanation
Of how you, a humble virgin,
Would conceive by the Holy Spirit
A child to be named Jesus,
The Son of the Most High God.

Mary, you must have been astounded
By the news the messenger brought.
We are told how you calmly accepted
The role you would play henceforth,
But you must have wondered about it
Long after Gabriel departed.

Did you keep the good news to yourself
Or did you hug your secret as a mother-to-be
Holds for a precious while
The knowledge that she is pregnant
And dwells with joy on the wonder of it all?

But even the angel's message
Did not make you forget
The joy of your elderly cousin
Who was now pregnant for six months.

Gabriel did not ask you to call on her
But there would have been reasons
Why you wished to do so:
To help her out in her last awkward months
And to let her in on your great secret.
Who better to share your news
Than this good woman
Who was so blessed by God?

MARY VISITS ELIZABETH

Women have a special way of sharing
Moments of great joy and sorrow.
A reaching out, an empathy,
A wordless sympathy.

With joyful anticipation
You set off on your journey
From your home in Nazareth
Through the hill country of Judaea,
Feeling only a sweet impatience
With the necessary stops
That broke your excited haste
To reach your cousin's house.

I would love to have been there
To see you wrap your arms around Elizabeth
And hear your words of congratulation!
What smiles and tears you must have shared
As loving glances lingered on each face.
And Elizabeth, before you had time
To tell her your good news,
In a prophetic outburst
Made you immediately aware that she knew
You were already the mother of her Lord,
And overwhelmed with joy your cousin told you
That as soon as she heard your greeting
The child within her jumped with gladness.

THE BIRTH OF JOHN THE BAPTIST

Were you there, Mary, at the birth of John?
Luke does not mention your presence
But I cannot believe you'd have left Elizabeth
At the time she most needed you.
I have a feeling that when telling your story later on
You concentrated on Elizabeth's great event,
Not mentioning your own participation
In those hours of glory.

You would have rejoiced with her neighbours
And kinsfolk, and marvelled at the insistence
Of your cousin, who said her baby would be called John
As Gabriel announced it would be.

Ignoring the crowd's disapproval
(For the name John came strange to their ears)
Zechariah wrote 'John' on the tablet
And immediately his voice returned.

What a clamour then followed
As friends found themselves
Witnesses to the works of the Lord!
What wonders they envisaged for the child!

But Zechariah, now filled with the Spirit,
Proclaimed as had been foretold:
'You, my child, will be called prophet
Of the Most High God. You will go ahead
Of the Lord, to prepare his road for him…'

And now Mary, your work being done,
You returned to Nazareth to await the birth
Of the Promised One, your son.

THE PROMISED ONE

There must have been many weeks
Of quiet discussion between Mary and Joseph
When the order came from Caesar Augustus
That a census be taken of the people in his Empire;
How to get to Bethlehem? What provisions to take?
Would Mary be able for the long journey
From Nazareth? (For now she was uncomfortably
Big with her child.) How would they manage
If she gave birth along the way?

In spite of their misgivings, one thing they knew,
They must obey the Emperor's Decree.
And so the young couple set out
In the company of friends and strangers
All going to Bethlehem to be enrolled.

And while in that city Mary gave birth,
In the gloomy starkness of a stable.

So that's how the Greatest Story ever told began!
The humble beginnings of the Saviour of the world,
God's Son, would be a sign to the proud and haughty,
To those in power or with authority,
In Church or State, that the Kingdom of Heaven
Belongs first to the lowly, and
If further proof were needed it was to the lowly,
The shepherds, whose conditions
Were not much better than the sheep they guarded,
That an angel came to tell them
That Christ, the Lord, was born,
And described how he was to be recognised.

JESUS IS PRESENTED IN THE TEMPLE

To fulfil the Jewish law of purification
Mary and Joseph went to Jerusalem
Taking the Child with them
To present him to the Lord,
Offering as a sacrifice a pair of turtle doves.

And while they were in the Temple
Simon, a devout and holy man
Whom the Holy Spirit had promised
That he would not die before he had seen
The Messiah,
Was inspired to come within,
And seeing the young couple with the child
Took the baby in his arms and gave thanks
That he had now seen the salvation of God's people.

And as Simon blessed him
He told Mary
That her heart would be broken
By the unnamed suffering
Her child would experience.

THE PROPHETESS ANNA

Through your constant prayers and fasting,
God rewarded you by making known
As you worshipped in the Temple
That the child present was He
Who was to set his people free.

And not content to keep
The Good News to yourself,
In your great joy you quickly
Spread the word to all around.

Widowed for many years,
The Lord had blessed you
With a new vocation.

THE ANNUAL PILGRIMAGE TO JERUSALEM

Year after year, Mary and Joseph
Went with the child to Jerusalem
To celebrate the Passover Festival.
This must have been a journey
Fraught with worry: the expense,
Joseph's precious savings near an end.
But withal, there would be holy anticipation
And joyful thoughts at the prospect
Of meeting with and talking to old friends,
The excitement at seeing the gathering crowd
As they neared Jerusalem,
The babble of foreign voices so loud
That Mary and Joseph would be hardly able
To hear each other speak.
And Jesus, a typical boy, getting tired
Of adult conversation, slipping away
To be with his young friends,
Giggling at some boyish joke
Or making others laugh
At his now well-known pranks
And exuberant behaviour.
But Mary and Joseph were well content
To leave the boy so;
He was young and must be allowed
The freedom of other company.
And with these thoughts
They happily faced the journey home,
Discussing with their many friends
All that happened in Jerusalem.

THE FINDING OF JESUS IN THE TEMPLE

Oh, I know, Mary and Joseph, how you felt
At the heart-stopping moment when you realised
Your son was not among the youthful company.
I, too, have undergone those awful hours
When our daughter, a thoughtful, loving child,
Failed to return home at the promised time
One agonising summer night.
We, too, sought help from neighbours,
City streets were scoured by police,
Hospitals phoned in case of accident;
And as the long hours brought no news
The silent screaming of our hearts
Rent the heavens with sobbing prayers
For the safe return of our beloved child.

I'll not go into detail of what happened –
Just to say she returned safely home,
The reason for the long and unexpected delay
Was later explained and because we had
Our child safely with us again, our chiding words
Were cut short by our prayerful gratitude.
But even now, remembering that awful night
I do not think our daughter fully understood
What we went through, what thoughts of horror
Filled our minds as to her fate.

And so I share with you that heart-stopping moment
When you both realised your son was nowhere to be found.

Your friends comforted you by saying
He can't have gone far, he's too sensible,
He must be somewhere around.
But deep down in your hearts you felt this awful dread;
Your child was lost, he might even be dead!
And as you returned to Jerusalem
Peering closely at every child along the way,
Hoping, praying, in drowning agony you thought
What hope was there in finding him
Through the still-crowded city streets?
(For many wealthy visitors would have stayed on.)
And yet you kept on asking questions
From total strangers that you met:
Had they seen this boy, and you described
His size and told his age, what he wore,
The colour of his hair, and more.
And some, compassionate, murmured sympathetic sounds,
While others, indifferent, merely glanced
At your tired faces, and went their way.
And then, as a last resort, you sought out the Temple,
And without much hope you entered,
And in the sacred gloom
You could make out a group of people.
Shading your eyes you neared the group
And heard the low-voiced murmurs,
But clearly above the adult sounds
A questioning young voice was raised
And your tired hearts leaped:
The voice could only be your son's.

Caught in a world between heaven and earth
And aware, perhaps for the first time,
Of his close connections with God,

Your son was unable to fully appreciate
What he had put you through.
He had enjoyed being able to discuss
With the teachers of the Law
The meaning of the Scriptures,
And his face was now aglow
With the excitement of it all.

His straying from the homebound group
Had been a thoughtless act,
A reflection of his lack of years
But more so of his humanness.
And we, dwelling on this one mishap,
Cannot help but smile at his boyish venture:
Though Son of God, he was truly one of us.

JOHN THE BAPTIST AND JESUS

I often wonder did Jesus and John
Ever meet during their youthful years.
Would they have met in Jerusalem
At the annual Passover Feast?
I imagine this would have happened.
They were cousins, so
Perhaps they were friends.

John's aged parents may have died
Before he set out on the mission
That he was destined to fulfil:
To prepare the way for the Lord.
And the multitude who gathered
To listen to his words, were eager
For some spiritual advice,
And that advice is as relevant to us now
As it was to the people back then:
'Share what you have with those less well off,
Do not cheat or charge more than you should,
Rob no one by violence, accuse no one falsely,
And don't desire more than you need.'

People wondered about John.
His actions and his words
Were not like those of anyone they knew;
He must be the Messiah they were expecting.
But John explained just who he was
And whom they were soon to see.
His preaching pleased many of his listeners
But it also disturbed those in power,

And because Herod could not live with truth
And the message that John had preached,
He threw him in prison, beyond reach.

THE TEMPTATION OF JESUS

When you were tempted, Jesus,
By the devil in the desert,
You were at your most vulnerable.
You had been alone for forty days,
And were hungry, thirsty and tired.
What would you have given
For a comfortable place to rest
Out of the scorching sun,
For a meal, or even some bread?

The devil, clever creature, knew the scriptures
And tried to use them to make you break.
Did he want his suspicions confirmed
That you were really the Son of God?
Or was it an attempt to make you seek
God's special intervention?

Seeing how truly human you were,
Subject to temptations and weaknesses,
Gives us hope that we too
Might persevere and resist
When temptations come before us.

JESUS' FIRST PUBLIC APPEARANCE

Jesus, it took some courage
To stand up in the synagogue in Nazareth,
To interpret the words of Isaiah
And apply them to yourself.
And that courage you received
From the Spirit of the Lord.
The words that flowed from your lips
Had their impact upon those gathered there,
Yet they could not accept that a son of Joseph
Could be so eloquent, so able to inspire.

But you, heedless of their reaction,
And knowing their expectations,
Said quite simply that a prophet
Is never welcomed in his home town.

(Is not the same begrudgery demonstrated
Today, in the world all around us:
Some 'ordinary person' rises from the ranks
And friends and neighbours are aggrieved.
Initially, they may be pleased
With the elevation of 'one of ourselves',
And then comes the jealousy and envy,
The need to 'take down a peg'.)

But what really maddened the crowd
Was when you reminded them
That in trying to limit your healing and preaching
They were calling upon themselves
The fate of their ancestors,

In the days of Elijah and Elisha.
And so they tried to push you over a cliff,
But the Spirit saved you
And you walked away.

JESUS HEALS SIMON'S MOTHER-IN-LAW

You left the synagogue in Capernaum
To go to Simon's house.
It seems you were a friend of Simon
Before you called him to be your disciple,
And you must have known his family well,
Being always sure of a welcome.
But on this occasion Simon's mother-in-law
Couldn't attend you, being too ill.
The family, aware of your power over ailments,
Spoke in hope that somehow she'd be made well.
And so it happened.

What delight and wonder greeted
This change in her condition!
The excitement as Simon's mother-in-law
And his wife set about preparing a meal
That would do honour to the occasion.
And then there was your bed to prepare,
For you were staying on to continue
Your work of healing.

At break of dawn you left the town
To seek a quiet place in which to pray,
But the people discovered where you were
And urged you to stay.
Then you reminded them of your mission:
To preach the Good News to every town along the way,
And so you set out to do just this
At the start of another love-filled day.

A DOUBLE REWARD

Nobody likes being caught in a crowd,
Being pressed all around, unable to break free,
And it's specially hard if the crowd recognises in you
A person of fame, someone they can look up to;
They need to get near you to shake your hand,
To engage in conversation, however brief,
And if that famous person is one
Who has good news for them
Or of whom it is said has the power to heal,
Then how hungrily the people move
Ever closer to the centre of their hope.
And so you sought a solution:
You asked Simon to push his boat off a little
From the shore
While you got in and told the crowd
The News they longed to hear.

There was a double reward in store
For your friend Simon and his fishing partners.
He and the others had spent a fruitless night
Fishing, but you, Jesus, made a simple request:
'Push the boat out further to the deep water
And you and your partners let down your nets
For a catch.' And they did as they were told.

Simon, overcome by the extraordinary richness
That followed, and recognising his own sinfulness,
And something of your Godliness
Fell on his knees in humble gratitude.
And now you gave him and his friends their second gift,
Their real vocation: 'Follow me.'

THE LETTER OF THE LAW

So many of us like to live
By the letter of the law
When it comes to religious practice.
There's a certain security in surrounding
Ourselves with walls of 'dos' and 'don'ts',
Which comfortably restrict us
To a quiet and easy life.
We want no gaps through which
We might see there is another way to live,
The only way to be.

Jesus, you must have been wearied
And frustrated at the number of times
You were taken to task by the teachers of the Law
For what appeared to them
Your apparent indifference to rules and regulations.
Healing on the Sabbath was seriously disapproved of:
As when you healed the man with the paralysed hand.
The teachers of the Law and some Pharisees
Were so filled with rage that you could outwit them
They discussed among themselves how they could undermine
your authority
And weaken your influence over the people.

LOVE YOUR ENEMIES

It is difficult, Lord, to love your enemies,
Those who have hurt you deeply,
Cheated or slandered you,
Perhaps caused the death of someone
You loved dearly.

And yet, Lord, you ask of us nothing
That you, yourself, were not always
Prepared to do,
And which you did with overflowing love
Right through to your last days on earth.

To make it easier for us to understand
Your command, you remind us
That God is good to the ungrateful
And the wicked,
So we have no alternative
But to do likewise.

Not easy, Lord,
We can only try!

NEVER FAITH LIKE THIS

Jesus, you had some surprises along the way!
The unexpected faith of the Roman officer
Who believed implicitly in your power to heal
His servant, and who felt unworthy of the honour
Your visit to his house would do him;
Neither did he feel worthy to meet you personally,
And so he sent friends to tell you
To travel no further, but just give the order
And his servant would be well, explaining
That he knew what it was to have authority
And how he expected his orders to be carried out.
He was equally sure that if you gave the order
His servant would immediately get well.

Such faith from such an unexpected quarter
Led you to exclaim to the crowd around you:
'I have never found faith like this,
Not even in Israel!'

And when the messengers went back
To the officer's house
They found the servant well.

I've often found myself pondering
On the sequels to many such stories.
We are not told of the overwhelming joy
That must have filled the hearts
Of the whole household
In that officer's home;
What took place to celebrate

The miraculous recovery of the servant?
Did all convert to the teaching of this new Preacher
Of whom they had heard so much?
I'd like to think that for them life changed,
That the Divine Intervention
Brought them a new and greater happiness.

God intervenes in my life many times
I have no doubt, but do I benefit
By the intervention in the way I might,
Or do I find myself looking in other directions
To see how others fare,
Seeing the mote in their eyes
But not the beam in mine?

JESUS RAISES A WIDOW'S SON

When we read this story
How many of us wish
You had been around
When a beloved relative died –
To see your face full of pity,
Our pain reflected in your eyes,
And then your hand outstretched
To touch our dead
With words 'Arise'.

But miracles do not occur like that;
The miracle is, that at some stage
Early or late, we get the grace
To accept that the time had come
For our dear ones to join you
In the Kingdom prepared for them.

WOMEN ACCOMPANY JESUS

What an extraordinary sight
It must have been to see you, Jesus,
Travelling through the towns and villages
With women disciples accompanying you
As well as the Twelve
Whom you had specially selected.

You must have been aware
That many were scandalised
By such behaviour.
And yet you took that risk
For you wanted the world to know
That all who loved and followed you,
Regardless of gender, creed or class,
Were your disciples,
And this truth you bore in your gentle, loving way
Throughout your public life.

JESUS CALMS A STORM

You used the lake to get from one place to another,
Sometimes to avoid the crowds
That continually pressed upon you;
On one occasion you used the lake
As a 'platform' from which to speak
To the people who hungered for your Word.

But on one journey when you wished to cross
To the other side of the lake,
Total weariness sent you to sleep,
A sleep so deep that the storm
Which suddenly arose failed to wake you up,
Even when the boat began to fill with water.

The danger became so great
That your disciples woke you up
With screams of terror,
Their terror, I imagine, not expressed
In words of gentleness
But in screams accompanied by hysterically
Shaking you awake.

Then the question was put to your friends:
'Where is your faith?'
Yes, where indeed is *our* faith
When the wind and the storm
Rock the boat that is our Church?

FAITH AMIDST DESPERATION

A faith, strengthened perhaps by desperation,
Moved Jairus, ruler of the synagogue,
To fall at Jesus' feet and beg him
To cure his dying daughter.
But in the midst of all the commotion
Generated by the arrival of the ruler,
A woman, unnoticed by the crowd,
Pushed her way to where Jesus was.
This woman had suffered from severe bleeding
For twelve long years; now she was destitute,
Having spent all her money on doctors
Who failed to heal her.

She had heard of Jesus and how he healed so many.
She would not directly ask him for a cure:
A touch of his garment would see her well.
Of this she was most sure.

Before she could steal back
Anonymously through the crowd
She heard his voice: 'Who touched me?'
A bewildered Peter said, 'The people all around
Are pressing on you', and privately
He must have thought, 'What a foolish question!'
But Jesus felt power had gone out of him
To the person who had touched him,
And the woman, knowing she had been found out,
Came forward, trembling,
And threw herself at the feet of Jesus.
Looking at her with love and compassion he said,
'Your faith has made you well. Go in peace.'

While he was speaking, a further commotion
Was caused by the arrival of a messenger
From the house of Jairus.
'Your daughter has died,' he said to the father.
'Don't bother the Teacher any longer.'
But Jesus overheard the words and said,
'Only believe and she will be well.'
And he directed his steps to the house,
The crowd following, eager to see
The result of such amazing words.

None but Peter, James and John
And the child's parents
Were allowed to witness
The resurrection of the child.
Taking her by the hand, Jesus called out,
'Get up, my child', and she got up at once
To the astonishment of those around.

HEALING POWER

When Jesus gave power to his disciples
To heal the sick as well as to preach
The Kingdom of God to all the people,
He surely did not intend to restrict
The gift of healing to his disciples
For that age alone,
And yet this gift of healing
So freely given
Has been neglected
Down through the ages.

Many people are gifted
With the power of healing
But do not know how to exercise it
Or, knowing, fail to do so
Lest they be thought of as charlatans
Who exploit the vulnerabilities
Of the afflicted.

We must reclaim
This most precious and unused gift –
A gift that this world of ours
Needs so much.

'WHO DO YOU SAY THAT I AM?'

I would like to believe
That I ponder this question
Seriously many times in life,
But the reality is I accept the answer
That Peter gave: 'You are God's Messiah.'
But not much real thought is given
To the question specifically asked of me.

Now I'll try to respond:
'You are the Son of God
Who took on human form
To be with us in the world we live in,
With all its ups and downs,
Its joys and sorrows.
You were so like us you could not be
Distinguished from other young people
As you grew up in your hometown.
Nothing about you marked you out
For the greatness of the Mission
You were to undertake;
A person like us in all things but sin.

But the time came for you to fulfil
The will of your Father: to preach,
Convert, and then to die for us.
Your love so boundless for each one of us
That if I were the only person for whom
It was necessary to give up your life
You would have willingly done so.
And this great thought
I'll ponder on until I die.'

'HE DOESN'T BELONG TO OUR GROUP'

How cosy it is to belong
To a group we can relate to,
One that makes us feel secure
In our own beliefs,
Never looking outward
To see if others are engaged
In the building of the Kingdom.

What right have these others
To preach, to convert or to heal?
We ignore them, or query
Their authority, their actions.
Exclusivity is our aim.

But, Jesus, you would have none of this;
So when your disciples tried to stop a man
Who was doing work in your name
You cautioned them with these words:
'Whoever is not against you is for you.'

JESUS TRUSTS US

What trust you had in the seventy-two
To let them go ahead of you!
Today we would think, how qualified
Were these ordinary people to preach,
To utter such amazing words as
'The Kingdom of God has come'.

Who would trust these ordinary seventy-two
To pass on the Word of God?
Who would take seriously their power
To heal the sick and afflicted?
But you, Jesus, trusted them.
Something in your words and actions,
In your utter goodness and sincerity,
Must have filled the hearts and minds
Of these missionaries, which enabled them
'To gather in the harvest'
With the confidence only you
Could have inspired.

And how your face shone with happiness
When they returned to tell what they had done!
You would have embraced them one by one,
Thanking your Father for showing you and them
How well his work was being fulfilled,
And then, privately, because others were around,
You told them how many prophets and kings
Wanted to see what they had seen
And to hear what they had heard,
But for them that was not to be.

THE GOOD SAMARITAN

A teacher of the Law tried to trap you
By asking what he must do
To receive eternal life.
And you replied: 'What do the Scriptures say?'
To which he responded:
'Love the Lord your God with all your heart,
With all your soul, strength and mind,
And love your neighbour as yourself.'
And you replied, 'You are right.
Do this and you will live.'

To justify his own beliefs the lawyer asked,
'Who is my neighbour?'
Little did he expect to hear the story
Of the Good Samaritan!
A Samaritan, despised by Jews
And trusted by none, being held up
As a good example of how all should behave
Towards the weak and broken!

Jesus, you were always full of surprises!
How this lawyer's comfortable beliefs
Must have been shaken as he pondered
On your words: 'Go, do the same as he.'

MARTHA AND MARY

Martha was eagerly preparing
A meal for you,
Her aim being to give you the best.
How annoyed she was to see Mary sitting down,
Heedless of the many tasks undone,
And you seemingly unaware
Of the busy hands and feet,
The flushed and tired face.

At length, provoked into a remonstrance
And barely able to keep the frustrated
Tears from brimming over,
She commanded you to tell her sister
There was work for her to do.

'Martha, Martha,' you would have said
In the softest coaxing way,
(For how could you have spoken otherwise,
You, who were so gentle and understanding)
And taking her by the hand
You would have slowed down
Her anxious heartbeat
To remind her there were greater things
In store for her. She too would be
His disciple, as Mary, even now,
Was thoughtfully learning to be.

MOMENTS WITH GOD

How often the disciples came
Upon Jesus deep in prayer,
That prayer so necessary to keep
In touch with God, the Father,
And to ask for strength
For the day's work ahead.

By his example Jesus showed us
That we need those moments with God:
To help us to resist
The weaknesses of the flesh;
To strengthen us for the times ahead,
To give us courage and hope to go on.

Above all they give us the joy
Of knowing that we are loved by God,
And being so loved we must extend
This love that envelops us to others,
Regardless of religion
Social or other differences,
And by acting thus we are helping in the work
Of building the Kingdom of God.

AN INVITATION FROM A PHARISEE

It was not the first time Jesus had received
An invitation to a meal from a Pharisee.
The Pharisees belonged to a religious party
That adhered strictly to the Law of Moses,
To which had been added on through the centuries
Rules and regulations thought necessary
To increase the fervour of their faith.
Jesus sometimes chose to ignore these rules,
And this upset the Pharisees,
Who laid traps and tried to catch him out
By saying something they regarded as wrong.

Jesus did not refuse the invitation
Though he was aware of the underlying motives.
This Pharisee was loved by him
As were all those who crowded around him,
Whether they agreed with him or not.
But loving people as he did
And prepared to die for them, as he would,
Did not prevent him from seeing through
The veneer of their spirituality,
Where appearances counted more
Than love of God or neighbour,
And injustice was cloaked
By ostentatious charity.
Seeing how these religious people acted,
He took them to task for their hypocrisies.
Yet, even as he spoke he would have yearned
For a change of heart, a change that would
Make them turn to the Life

He was offering them,
The only Life that mattered.

Some of those Pharisees
Were intrigued by what they had heard
And were drawn to his presence,
But yet they went away dissatisfied
Because his words disturbed them
And shook the customs
They had religiously observed.
I wonder did many ponder his words
And eventually turn back to follow him!

TRUST IN GOD

It is natural to worry about the future,
For parents to worry about their children,
For religious leaders to worry about their flock,
For business people to worry about profits,
For workers to worry about job security.

We all worry about things
At one time or another in our lives.
Sometimes we worry needlessly,
Anticipating trouble or problems
That may never come to pass.
And Jesus, understanding our human nature,
Sympathises fully with us.

Worry can take over our lives
But it won't add one single day
To our life's span, nor will it guarantee
That we'll have time to enjoy the result
Of such an investment of stress and strain.
Relax! Trust in God.
It is right that we should earn our living
And look to the welfare of those in need,
But piling up riches for oneself
Is of no benefit to others;
You cannot take them with you after death
And the money you hoarded while on earth
Will not provide riches for you in heaven.

FAITHFUL AND UNFAITHFUL SERVANTS

It can be frightening
When we realise that each of us
Has responsibilities to others
In our daily lives.

Do we fulfil our duties with care
And love? Or are we heedless
Of how we act, as long
As we ourselves don't suffer?

Jesus is hard on neglectful leadership,
Whether it is a minor or a major transgression.
Careless parenting, religious leaders
Unfaithful to their vocation,
Unjust employers, dishonest employees,
Corrupt political leaders,
Ungrateful and neglectful children –
Each of us has to answer to God
For our failures to use our talents
In the roles allotted to us.

And there is this reminder:
The more we have been given
The more is expected of us.

JESUS HEALS A CRIPPLED WOMAN

When I re-read the Gospel I compare it
To walking through a beautiful countryside:
Each time I walk I see the same landscape,
But nature, never idle, has painted
Some hill or mountain with fresh colour,
Or outlined more clearly the shape
Of a deep blue lake, or flooded
To a foaming cataract
The placid, meandering summer stream.

In the same way when I re-read the Gospel
New meanings come to light,
New insights brighten up the pages,
Which make me pause, to reflect:
I was there before, but now
I see it differently.

And when I re-read this story
Of the crippled woman
I realise what Jesus wished to demonstrate:
This woman, unknown, so lowly
She did not merit in the report
The one thing that belonged to her –
     Her name,
Mattered very much to the compassionate healer
Who picked her sickly, stooping figure
From out of the crowd of women
Massed at the back of the synagogue.
And, hearing him call, she moved
With halting footsteps to where he sat

And told her she was free
From her crippling illness.
Then the tender, kind and loving Preacher
Laid his hands upon her,
And to the astonishment of the crowd
She straightened up, and no longer trying
To revert to anonymity because of her gender
And her cruel ailment, she immediately
Gave rein to grateful words of praise.

But this strange event went hard
With the ruler of the synagogue.
Learned as he was, he did not see
That in this act Jesus was implementing
The words of Isaiah
'The Spirit of the Lord is upon me…
To set free the oppressed',
And so he railed against the fact that the holiness
Of the Sabbath was violated by the far
From urgent healing of this lowly, unknown woman.
But Jesus accused him
And like-minded people present
Of hypocrisy, by pointing out
That even they, hypocrites as they were,
Would not hesitate to untie their donkey
On the Sabbath and bring it
To a place where it could drink.
(Though strictly speaking, and in adherence
To their Law, this kind of thing was frowned upon.)

This miracle makes me wonder why the ruler
Was not dumbfounded by the event he had just seen!
Was he so busy preparing a blistering response,

So heedless of the rejoicing, awe-filled crowds,
So incensed, that no miracle,
Nothing he had heard, would make him see
That here in his very presence
Was the fulfilment the Jewish people
Had for centuries longed to witness?

JESUS' LOVE FOR JERUSALEM

Such great love welled up in your heart
For the city of Jerusalem
That you gave vent to words
Which cannot fail to touch
The hearts of those who ponder
On the emotional outburst
That made you compare
Your tender care to that
Of a mother hen who gathers
All her chicks under the protection
Of her wings.

Your eyes must have filled with tears
To see so much love frustrated
By stubborn beliefs and attitudes;
You saw that little had changed
From the times when God's messengers
And prophets were stoned or killed
By the ancestors of those around you.

You knew your turn would come
And your heart was broken,
Not for your future suffering,
But because people were so deaf
To the Message that God had given you
To deliver to them.

'WHEN YOU GIVE A LUNCH OR A DINNER'

Lord, how can I possibly do
What you ask of me?
'When you give a lunch or a dinner
Do not invite your friends or relatives;
Instead invite the poor, the crippled,
The lame and the blind…'

Lord, I like giving parties,
But the truth is I invite only
My relatives and friends.
I have never once invited
To sit at my table
The poor, the crippled,
The lame and the blind.
Nor can I see myself
Doing such a thing!

How then can I face you
When I come before
Your judgement seat?
Please do not say
'I do not know you'.
You see, I try to meet
Your demand in other ways.
Please accept my good intent.

THE LOST SHEEP

Whenever we go astray or deviate
From the path that leads to you,
No matter how long we have been away
You are always watching for us
With arms outstretched
To welcome us warmly to your heart.

You never give up on anyone
No matter how sinful they have been,
Though some have given up on you
And ignore the thought of a future life
Which they believe does not exist.

If we do not change our ways
And return to you, you seek us out;
And no matter how long it takes,
What wearied days and weeks and years
Are spent in searching,
You find us in the end
And welcome us back with joyful tears.

THE KINGDOM OF GOD IS WITHIN US

Our tendency is to look for signs and wonders
In order to bolster our weakening faith;
We hear of moving statues,
Of heavenly appearances,
And wonder are they real or fake.
Some of us scoff at the idea
That God through these 'events'
Is delivering some message
We have not already heard,
While others glory in the thought
That God's presence is made manifest
In that particular place or sculpted work,
And by these 'occurrences' their faith increases
Until the novelty of the event
Grows dim by the cares and worries
Of their humdrum lives.

But you, Jesus, remind us
That the Kingdom of God is within us all;
The power and the glory
Of what awaits us as our final Reward
We have in great measure here on earth.
You are there, God, in the people
We interact with each day.
No one is deprived of this Divine gift,
But first we need to see it in ourselves
And then, reflecting on this wonder,
See it in every human being whom
You, with infinite love, created.

INGRATITUDE

Eaten bread is soon forgotten!
When it comes to personal experience
Where we have done someone a favour
And that favour has been taken for granted,
Or worse still, we aren't even thanked,
We are upset, and we aren't slow in relating
To others what an ungrateful person
The favoured one is.

And often we use this experience of ingratitude
To stop us from doing further acts of kindness
To people who seek our help,
And we feel justified in doing so.

The ingratitude of the lepers you cured
When only one of them, a despised Samaritan,
Returned to thank you,
Did not prevent you, Jesus, from curing
Other people who approached you
Or followed you along the way.

We, too, are guilty of wounding
Ingratitude to you, our God.
In the course of our daily lives
We are quick to ask for favours
And are disappointed
When there is no immediate response.
And yet when our prayers are granted,
Whether immediate or delayed,
Our gratitude to you doesn't often follow,
And if it does, how deep, how prolonged
Is that prayer of thanks to you?

TRUSTING FAITH

Trusting, simple faith is often mocked
By those who think they know better!
The still figure of the old man
At the altar, his eyes fixed
On the Tabernacle in reverent adoration,
The old woman fingering her beads
In the remote darkness of the church,
The little child who repeats its prayers
At the bedside or at the knees
Of a loving parent –
What do all of these know
Of the depth, the wonder and grandeur of God?

What theology have they studied?
What in-depth reading of Scriptures
Have they done? What intensive research
Of ancient tomes have they accumulated
To make them understand who God is
And what he has done for all of us?

The answer is an emphatic 'none',
But their simple, trusting faith,
Like the children whom Jesus called
To him, when his disciples
Would have pushed them to one side,
Is what he desires more than all
The wealth of knowledge gathered
By eminent scholars and academics.

As Jesus reminds us: 'Whoever does not
Receive the Kingdom of God
Like a child, will never enter it.'
A kindly warning to which we must pay heed.

JESUS SPEAKS ABOUT HIS DEATH

Few of us wish to be reminded of death.
And when we're told of the imminent death
Of a loved one or of ourselves
How we rebel against such news!
Denial of the truth followed by anger
And fuming impotence are replaced
By a feeling of desolation
That such a thing should be allowed to happen.
The whole thing is beyond our comprehension!

So when Jesus spoke to his disciples
About his death, explaining that all
That had been written by the prophets
About the Son of Man was going to be fulfilled,
Detailing to them the horrors he would undergo,
But that three days after his death
He would rise again,
Instead of the expected anger and outrage
That should have followed this announcement
It seems that denial was their only comfort,
Because how could they understand
That such a tragic ending should happen
To their beloved Teacher
After all he had done for others?

JESUS AND ZACCHAEUS

Zacchaeus must have heard a lot about you, Jesus,
And some door in his mind was opened
To the tales of goodness, mercy and love
That he had heard about you everywhere he went.

He must have longed to meet you,
You, who were so different from the man
He now knew himself to be.
He, a tax-collector, not caring
Who suffered, as long as he had wealth.
And when he saw the gathering crowd
He knew at once that you were in their midst,
And rushing towards you he was frustrated
By his small height and quickly climbed a tree
And balanced himself on the strongest branch
That overhung the road you were travelling on.

He only came to look, but little
Did he think that you would lift your head
And see him peering down at you,
Then call to him to hurry down
As you were going to stay
In his house that very day.

No wonder the people grumbled
When you chose this man
Whom they despised and thought
Unworthy of your company,
And Zacchaeus, now totally transformed
By the grace of your presence,

Made promises that you knew he would fulfil –
The outcast was no longer outcast
Because you had reached out to him
And he would sit at table with you
In spite of protests from the crowd.

JESUS WEEPS OVER JERUSALEM

It wasn't easy for your friends to see you weeping.
Always you had kept your spirits up
With encouraging words to those who followed you,
Those who listened to the Good News
You wished to share with them.

But there must have been times when you sought
Some hidden place and let the tears fall unseen,
Weariness opening the dam you had kept closed
While you were with the crowds,
Sad that even the leaders,
Who knew the Scripture well,
Failed to recognise that the One among them
Was He of whom the prophets had foretold.

Now as you looked down upon your beloved city
Your heart was broken over the failure
Of her citizens to understand the peace
That only comes from God.
The enemies of Jerusalem would in time
Destroy the city and all its people.

If your words were listened to even then
And taken to heart by those in authority
I believe the city would have been saved
And what followed would have changed
The course of history.

QUESTIONING JESUS' AUTHORITY

Sometimes, Jesus, I have to laugh
At the way you answer questions
Put to you by the teachers of the Law.
You know when a question is asked
Sincerely, and when the Scribes and Pharisees
Are trying you to catch you out.
On one occasion the chief priest, no less,
And teachers of the Law, along with the Elders,
Questioned your right to speak in the way you did.
And you answered their question with
Another one: 'Did John's authority
Come from God or man?'

They huddled together like a team
Searching for an answer,
But in the end they failed to say
Where John's authority came from.
And your response was,
'If you cannot tell me, neither will I'.

But the teachers of the Law were not to be outwitted
By an 'unauthorised' preacher.
Next time they bribed some men to pretend
They were sincere, and sent them
To trap you with more questions.
How well they began by flattering you in words
That were really true had they but known it,
And then the trick one! 'Is it against our Law
To pay taxes or not?'
Straightaway you asked to be shown a silver coin.

'Whose face and name are these on it?'

'The Emperor's', they replied.

'Well then,' you said, 'pay the Emperor what belongs
To the Emperor and pay God what belongs to God.'

THE WIDOW'S OFFERING

Once more, Jesus, you showed us
How gifts to others are measured,
By your observation of those who dropped their gifts
Into the Temple treasury:
The wealthy gave of their abundance and so
Their offering caused them no great hardship;
But the poor widow who dropped in two copper coins
Gave all she had to live on.

You knew her great sacrifice would leave her
Destitute for some time, but
She was willing to endure deprivation,
And her generous act of love
Was greater in your eyes
Than all the gifts of the rich combined.

Thus the story of the widow's offering
Demonstrates to us in a simple way
That it is not how much we give
But the sacrifice entailed in giving.

TROUBLES AND PERSECUTIONS

It is with sadness and despondency
I listen to you speak
Of the troubles and persecutions to come.
Those times would be,
It seems to me, when your followers
Would be persecuted, put in prison,
Even killed for your name's sake.
And my sadness and despondency deepens
When I listen to or read about
The atrocities carried out
On each other by those
Who call themselves Christians.
What is it all about?
What answers can be given
For such evil-doing?

THE PLOT AGAINST JESUS

It must have upset the chief priests
And the teachers of the Law
To see you daily in the Temple
With the people gathered round
To hear the Good News.
And so they planned to kill you.
But the presence of so many
Frustrated their attempts at arrest.
They feared the people's anger
Should not be put to the test.

At night you'd go to the Mount of Olives
To think and rest and pray.
And here it was that Judas did
Betray you to your enemies.

JUDAS

What can one say of Judas?
He was selected from among
Many disciples by Jesus,
And Jesus had spent the whole night
Praying to the Father
Before the day he chose the twelve.

Jesus would have seen in the young man
A person worthy of his place
Among those whom he specially called
To pass on the Good News,
And Judas would have been drawn
To Jesus, because of who he was
And the words he spoke
(Though not fully understanding
That he was the One sent by God
To be the Saviour of the world).

The teacher's kind and gentle manner
Would have appealed to him;
He who had never been understood
As now he felt he was.
And when Jesus sent out the Twelve
To preach the Kingdom of God,
And to heal the sick and spread the Word,
He would have done so with joy
Knowing that Jesus had given them
The power and authority
To do what he asked them to do.
How long did it take for Judas
To succumb to the final temptation
To betray his Friend and Master?

THE LORD'S SUPPER

Lord, even in your last hours on earth,
And knowing all you had to face,
You did not overlook the annual
Celebration of the Passover.
As ever, you honoured all the rituals of old,
And in the act of honouring them
You gave them a richer meaning.

As you sat at table with your friends
You gave them to understand
That from now on they must share
All they had with others –
Love, the Good news, life itself.

And then came that great moment
When you took some bread
And gave each of them a piece
And said: 'This is my body
Which is given for you';
And when you handed around the wine
You said to them: 'This cup
Is God's new covenant sealed
With my blood, poured out for you.'

It was then that you revealed
That one among you, with whom you shared
Everything, was even now
Planning to betray you.

What terrible weakness is in us, Jesus,
When at the moment you are closest to us,
We can be guilty of betraying your love?
– Love that you pour out in abundance for us all.
Would the answer lie in the mystery
Of our redemption?

ARGUMENTS ABOUT GREATNESS

Isn't it a pity that we,
Political leaders, Church leaders,
Ordinary folk, do not concentrate
More on the words you spoke
To your disciples at the Last Supper?
Even they could not resist arguing
Among themselves as to which of them
Should be thought of as the greatest!

So many of us are caught up
With our own importance,
In the day-to-day activities
Of our lives,
That we forget completely
The significance of your words:
'The greatest one among you
Must be like the youngest,
And the leader must be like the servant…
I am among you as one who serves.'

You, God the Son, pronounced those words.
You made it clear that as you chose
The role of one who serves,
So also should we.
And yet so few of us choose
To take on the mantle of servant,
Preferring instead some power and stature.
How foolish we are indeed!

PETER

There was something very lovable about Peter:
Faithful follower of Jesus, always concerned
For his Master's safety, quick to give
Him advice when danger loomed,
Never slow to express his feelings
Of loyalty and the understanding he had
Of whom the Master was.

And when the Master warned him
That Satan would tempt him,
And that he hoped his faith
Would not fail him,
Peter exclaimed that he was ready
To go to prison for Jesus,
Even to die with him!

Then came the quiet words of Jesus:
'The cock will not crow tonight
Until you have claimed three times
That you do not know me.'

And so it turned out to be.
Peter denied his Master
And repented bitterly.

Yet this Peter, with all his weaknesses
And lovable virtues, was the man
Whom Jesus appointed as leader.
This should be a lesson to all
That though we may fall and break our word with him,

Not only once, but many times throughout our lives,
In all of us there are facets that can go to make
Qualities of leadership in roles, great or lowly,
And that he trusts us to carry them out
In the best way we can.

THE AGONY IN THE GARDEN

Unlike your friends
I do not stay behind
To watch and pray,
But follow your lonely figure
To the hard, unyielding rock
That juts up from the earth,
White and clear
Under the stark moonlight.

I see you
Clasp your hands
So tightly that the knuckles
Bare to bone;
Your skin, like bleached linen
Stretches thinly
Across a face
Pain-hollowed

As you beg your Father
For the help to drink
The cup of searing,
Tearing pain.
Your friends collapsed in sleep
As you lie, crushed with sorrow
Upon the rock,

Crying out,
Again and again,
'Father, if it is possible
Take this cup of suffering

Away from me,
This cup I dread to drink.'
And when I hear you add:
'Let it not be what I want
But what you want from me,'
I can do naught but weep...

Now as I stand and stare
At the gnarled and ancient olive trees
I wonder what would I have done
Two thousand years ago
If I had been among
That selected company.

Would I have slept
In fitful starts
Fearful of what
The night might bring?
Or would I
Have slunk away,
Courage disappearing
With the approaching day?

No use conjecturing
On what might have been.
I am here
And I am praying.

THE ARREST OF JESUS

It was night.
No crowd of believers was around
To prevent or interfere with his arrest.
Judas, for reasons we shall never understand,
Led a varied group of people, officers of the temple guard,
And elders, to the place where he knew full well
Jesus would have come to, to pray.
And so in the safety of a deserted garden
Whose ghostly trees formed strange shapes in the dark,
They came to arrest the man
Who had annoyed and frustrated them
For so long.

Now his hour had come
And victory was theirs at last!

Jesus,
Though he foretold in the Supper Room
That Judas would betray him,
Must nonetheless have been
Truly shocked at his treachery,
Especially as it was accompanied
By the kiss of friendship.

But sadder words were reserved
For the principals who were present;
They had not the courage to arrest him
While preaching in the Temple every day.
Now they approached him as if he were
Some evil felon, carrying swords

And clubs to use if necessary
Should he try to make a quick escape.

    Unresisting,
Jesus suffered the rough handling
Of his captors and was led away.

The first stop was at the High Priest's house,
And trailing far behind was Peter.
Seeing a bright fire in the centre
Of the courtyard, and feeling cold
And frightened, he drew near
(The heat might warm his trembling limbs
And help to drive away his fear)
And joined those who were sitting there.
They were not threatening people,
Just servants – he could deal with them.
But little did he expect that he would be
Recognised at once by a servant girl;
She had often seen him
In the company of Jesus,
And in a loud voice she exclaimed:
'This man I know to be a friend of Jesus.'

Jumping up in fright
He immediately denied
That he ever knew him.
But Peter was not left
Very long in peace;
Another man, with heavy irony,
Said to him: 'You too are one of them!'
To which Peter vehemently replied:
    'I am not!'

Later, a man who had been studying
Peter's face and form
And listening to his accent,
With great certainty said:
'There isn't any doubt who this man is.
I have seen him with Jesus
And I know from where he comes.'
Now Peter had heard enough!

He'd see to it that no one else
Would make such accusations,
And hoarse with fear he shouted:
'Man, I do not know
What you are talking about!'
And even as he spoke,
From the near distance
A cock, signalling the dawn,
Crowed loud and clear.

Jesus, who had gone on ahead,
Turned round and gazed at Peter,
Who remembered what the Lord had said:
'Before the cock crows
You will claim three times
That you do not know me.'
Overcome by what he had done
He left the crowd, while bitter tears
Flowed down his cheeks unchecked.

JESUS IS BROUGHT BEFORE THE COUNCIL

What was it that made self-righteous people
Accuse God's graced person
Of actions they knew deep down
To be utterly false?
As Jesus stood before the Council
He showed no fear,
But they were fearful of the word 'Messiah',
Because by his actions
He had brought about
What the prophets had foretold.

Now they had run out of accusations
That could stick when they brought Jesus
Before Pilate, going so far as to say
That they had heard him tell the people
Not to pay taxes to the Emperor,
When in fact he had emphatically stated
That they were to pay the Emperor his due
And pay God what belonged to him.

And these men who had studied the Scriptures
Were greatly disturbed by this preacher,
He the son of a carpenter, not qualified to preach,
Yet preaching and performing miracles
That they couldn't deny.
Pilate was mystified by their accusations
Which could not hold up in a court of law,
And so, refusing to condemn Jesus,
He sent him on to Herod.

Herod was pleased to see this man
Of whom he had heard so much.
He desired to see what made him tick,
What all the fame was about.
Perhaps he would perform a miracle,
Make his journey to Jerusalem worthwhile!

But Jesus answered him not a word,
And so the true feelings of Herod
Were exposed for what they were!
And as no one could expect to go unpunished
For such audacity, Herod urged the soldiers
To insult the man who stood before him
In any manner they so desired,
And he amused himself
By joining in their mocking.
Later, bored by no reaction
From the silent Jesus,
He sent him back to Pilate.

THE SCOURGING OF JESUS
AT THE PILLAR

Reflection on a Painting

Your face reflects the agonising pain
Of each gross act
Inflicted on your powerful frame:
A frame whose muscles
Once flexed and rippled
To the rhythmic sawing of timber
Or to the patient planing of uncouth wood
When you were provider
For that humble home in Nazareth;
A frame that was so finely tuned
For the energy required
To cover the length and breadth
Of your homeland,
When tired feet almost gave up
But were urged on further
By a loving zeal
To bring the Good News to the poor,
Liberty to the captive,
Sight to the blind
And freedom to the oppressed.

Now as you stand roped and captive,
Does this new excruciation
Allow you to remember those moments
When your eyes were blinded
By the spittle of those
Who mocked because you claimed
To be the Son of God?
Then led to the praetorium,

A questioning Roman governor
Made fearful and uneasy by your replies
Sought to have you freed,
But overwhelmed by the clamour of the mob
Who cried out for your death,
Ordered this brutalising punishment.

Because you were God made man
Artists through the centuries
Have depicted you
As the stoic sufferer
Enduring with awful calm,
Each separate and cruel stroke
From whips
Fringed with bloody flesh;
But as I stand and gaze
At this passion painting
I see more clearly
Than I've ever seen before
How truly human you really were:

Tears of exquisite pain
Spurt in great globules
From eyes heavy lidded
By wearying hours of interrogation.
Betrayed, denied,
You stand forsaken,
Your lips in viscous grimace
No longer capable of speaking
Words of hope and love,
And that once so vibrant face,
Tortured into gaunt hollows,
Sinks heartbroken
In unutterable desolation.

PILATE ATTEMPTS TO SET JESUS FREE

Pilate, having ordered Jesus to be scourged,
Thought the people would be satisfied
With this punishment,
But the crowd that had now gathered
Must already have been primed to respond
In frenzied chorus: 'Kill him!
We want Barabbas freed instead!'

Pilate, taken aback by this response,
And knowing that Barabbas, a murderer,
Had been found guilty of inciting a riot in the city,
Was eager to set him free,
But weakly he yielded to the demands
Of that swelling angry mob,
And he handed Jesus over to those
Who sought his death.

JESUS IS CRUCIFIED

Jesus, if you were to be crucified today,
How many column inches would you get
In the newspapers? Would this extraordinary event
Reach the headlines on radio or TV?
Somehow, I feel it would!
Though the reporters might not understand
The nature of what happened,
The sheer horror if it all
Would bring it centre-stage.

Many thousands of books have been written
Over the centuries to explain more fully
Why you came on earth,
Why you endured such punishment,
Why you gave your life for us.
But if we ponder on the few notes taken
Two thousand years ago,
Describing the Event, all is there
That we really need to know.

On your way to the place called 'The Skull',
Where you were to be crucified,
A crowd of people followed you,
Among them women who were weeping loudly
At seeing you, their loving friend,
So cruelly and ignominiously treated.
And in spite of what you were going through
You turned around to give them
Words of comfort and advice.

You must also have looked with compassion
At Simon of Cyrene who happened
To be passing on his way to the city
And was ordered by the soldiers
To carry the cross with you,
Not to relieve you from the weight,
But for fear you might die along the way
And so not face what was to be
Your ultimate fate.

No one can possibly absorb
What you went through
On that fateful day,
How your love and forgiveness
Reached out to all,
Even to those who nailed you
To the cross.

THE DEATH OF JESUS

In your dying hours, nature
Altered its natural course.
The sun could no longer shine
Where the Creator's Son
Hung in disgrace;
And darkness fell to cover the shame
Of that awful scene.
The hour had now come
For you to hand over yourself
And the work you had accomplished
To your Father.
Nothing more was left to be done.
And dredging up the energy
For one last agonising gasp
You called out, 'Father!
In your hands I place my spirit!',
And as your head drooped slowly
Upon your blood-spattered chest
You died...

THE FAITHFUL FEW

You must have lifted your eyes from time to time
As your pain-wracked body hung on the cross
And looked around to see the faithful few
Who had followed you
On your agonising journey to the Mount.
Where were those who had been cured by you?
You would not have thought harshly of them
Or their ingratitude, but you must have been
Heart-sore, saddened by their lack of support
Now when you needed it most.

When your eyes lighted upon the faithful women
Who stood helplessly as you hung dying,
You were aware of the outpouring of love
In which they silently enveloped you,
And their fearless loyalty
Was balm to your wounded spirit.

Joseph of Arimathea, a good and honourable man,
Had asked permission from Pilate
To be allowed to bury you,
And the faithful women went with Joseph
To the tomb
To see where your body was being placed.
They knew they could not stay around
As the Sabbath was about to begin,
But before leaving they gazed once more
At your lonely tomb,
Peering through tear-filled eyes
At the massive stone which Joseph's men

Had rolled up to the opening.
Then they made their weary way homewards
To prepare the spices for your proper burial
After the Sabbath Day.

THE RESURRECTION

Darkness cloaked the empty streets
When your women friends left their homes
Carrying the prepared spices.
Nameless fears gripped them
As they passed by every shadowed alleyway,
And speaking in infrequent
And frightened whispers lest the strange shapes
That loomed ahead took life
And blocked their way to where you,
Their Beloved, lay,
They drew courage from each other's company.

Through the streets they went, silent
But for the swift shuffle of sandalled feet
And the swish of their ankle-length gowns,
And moving rapidly they reached the tomb.

To their amazement, the problem
That had filled their minds
Along the journey there:
Who would roll back the stone
So that they might complete
Their precious work?
Was resolved for them.
The stone was already rolled back
But your body was gone.
Puzzled and apprehensive,
They stood around,
When suddenly two men appeared.
Dazzled by their appearance they bowed low,

And heard the men say, 'Why do you look
Among the dead for one who is not here?
The one you seek has been raised from the dead.
Do you not remember while in Galilee
That he said, "The Son of Man
Must be handed over to sinful men,
Be crucified and three days later
Rise to life?" '

Remembering your words they accepted
What had happened as the truth;
They left the tomb and told the astounding news
To the eleven disciples
And the other followers present.

But their story was dismissed
As nonsense. Who could believe
What these women would say?
Hysterical, that's what they were.
Typical behaviour of women!
But some little doubt stirred in Peter.
Suddenly he left the chattering group
And raced to the tomb;
He saw nothing but linen wrappings.
Head nodding vigorously he muttered in awe:
'Ah, the women were right!'

Eyes sweeping the empty tomb
With one last lingering look,
He left to return to the others
With his confirmation
Of what had happened.

THE WALK TO EMMAUS

Desolate and totally shattered by what had happened,
Two followers of Jesus made their way home to Emmaus.
Dragging their weary bodies forward,
They talked about those recent awful days
And could make no sense of it at all.
And now life for them must return to what
It once had been before their Friend
Had shown them there was another Life.

Conscious of footsteps behind them
They slowed down to let the stranger pass,
But Jesus (for it was he) walked with them
And seeing how downcast they were
Asked what was troubling them.
Not recognising him they paused,
Amazed that he should be unaware
Of the strange things
That had recently occurred in Jerusalem.

Feigning ignorance he drew them out.
'What things?', and only eager
To share the news that broke their hearts,
Words flowed and would not be stilled
Until they had emptied their anguished minds
Of all the sorrows and frustrations
Which up to this had tormented
Their every waking moment.

Out it all came: their hopes for themselves
And for Israel. This man, Jesus,

Seemed so powerful that he could do anything,
And indeed he did many wonderful things.
They were certain he was a man
Sent from God, and look what had happened!
He was put to death like a common criminal!

Now there were all sorts of rumours around
That his body was missing from the tomb.
Some women came with the news first
But nobody took them seriously, and then
Some men went to the tomb
And came back with the same story.
So what were they to believe!

Then Jesus, chiding them gently, explained
The extraordinary happenings,
Referring to the prophecies that were made about himself
And how all these prophecies had now been fulfilled.
Coming near home, it seemed Jesus
Intended to walk further, but the couple
Persuaded him to stay overnight with them
As it was getting dark.
He readily agreed and supper was prepared.

Then something strange occurred.
Jesus, acting as host, pronounced the blessing,
And breaking the bread he gave each a piece.
Suddenly it all came back –
That other time when they sat at Supper.
This man was the Risen Jesus.
But even as their eyes were opened
Their Friend had disappeared.

No longer hungry,
And eager to spread the News,
They left the house
And swiftly made their way
To Jerusalem.

A FRIEND TO THE END

So now the story the disciples thought
Had ended, was really only beginning.
Jesus, their beloved Friend and Leader,
Had appeared to several followers
And, so that their faith in his resurrection
Might be more fully confirmed,
He appeared in the room
As the couple from Emmaus
Were relating their experience.

In their terror, for the apostles thought he was a ghost,
They scarcely heard his words:
'Peace be with you', words he had so often
Greeted them with in past encounters.
Allaying their terror, he invited them
To look at his wounded hands and feet;
To touch him so that they would know he was real.
And to banish any lingering doubts
He asked for food to eat.

After the meal he said once more
That anything that had been foretold
About him in the writings of the prophets
Had come true, and again he opened their minds
To understand the Scriptures.
Then he promised them 'Power from above'
Which they would receive
While waiting in Jerusalem.

Loyal to the end, he led them
From the city to Bethany.
There he raised his hands in blessing,
And as he did so he was taken up to heaven.
Heartened by his words and his promises
And by the blessed leave-taking
They returned joyfully to Jerusalem.